Contents

The Chessmaster

Anurag Anurag

1

Unraveling Threads

Detective James Reynolds was no stranger to difficult cases, but this one was beginning to take its toll on him. The murders that had shaken the small town of Millstone were not just gruesome—they were baffling. It seemed as if each new murder was another piece of a puzzle that refused to fit together.

Reynolds sat in his dimly lit office, staring at the corkboard on the wall. Red strings connected various locations on the map of Millstone, each marking the site of a murder. The dates of the killings were scribbled on sticky notes, stuck haphazardly around the edges of the board. No matter how much he stared at it, he couldn't make sense of it. The pattern—if there was one—eluded him.

He ran a hand through his hair, which was beginning to show more gray than brown, and leaned back in his chair with a heavy sigh. His eyes were tired, and his mind felt like it was running in circles, chasing after a ghost.

The door to his office creaked open, and Deputy Sarah Miller stepped inside, carrying two cups of coffee. She placed one on Reynolds' desk and sat down across from him, her expression one of concern.

"You look like hell, Sheriff," she said, taking a sip from her cup.

Reynolds chuckled dryly, though there was no humor in it. "I feel like it too. This case... it's getting under my skin, Sarah. I've never dealt with anything like this before."

Sarah nodded, her eyes flicking to the corkboard. "I know. It's like we're chasing shadows. Every time we think we've got something, it slips through our fingers."

Reynolds took a long drink of his coffee, letting the warmth spread through him. "There's got to be something we're missing. These murders... they can't be random. There's a connection here, something that ties them together, but I just can't see it."

Sarah leaned forward, resting her elbows on the desk. "What if it's not about the victims? What if the connection is in the timing?"

Reynolds frowned, considering her words. "What do you mean?"

"Well," Sarah began, choosing her words carefully, "I've been looking at the dates. The murders aren't happening close together, but they're not exactly spread out evenly either. It's almost like there's a rhythm to them—every few months, another murder."

Reynolds pulled the sticky notes from the board and laid them out on his desk in a line, the dates of the killings in clear view. "You might be onto something," he said, rubbing his chin thoughtfully. "But what does it mean? If there's a pattern in the timing, it could tell us something about the killer's motive or state of mind."

Sarah nodded. "Or maybe it's something more practical. Maybe the killer is waiting for specific circumstances—something only they know about—to strike."

Reynolds stared at the dates, trying to find some meaning in the sequence. But the more he looked, the more it seemed like just another random jumble. The frustration that had been simmering inside him for weeks began to boil over.

"Damn it!" Reynolds slammed his fist on the desk, making the coffee cups jump. "Why can't I figure this out?"

Sarah remained calm, though she flinched at the outburst. "Sheriff, we're doing everything we can. This isn't your fault. We just need to keep looking, keep digging."

Reynolds stood up and began pacing the room, his mind racing. "It's not enough, Sarah. We're running out of time. Every day that passes is another day that the killer could be planning their next move. And we're just sitting here, spinning our wheels."

"Then let's take a step back," Sarah suggested. "Maybe we're too close to this. We need to clear our heads, look at the case from a different angle."

Reynolds stopped pacing and turned to face her, his expression one of exhaustion and defeat. "I don't know how much more of this I can take, Sarah. I've never felt so... powerless."

Sarah stood and placed a reassuring hand on his shoulder. "You're not alone in this, Sheriff. We're a team. We'll figure this out together."

Reynolds looked into her eyes and saw the determination there, the same determination that had kept him going for so long. He nodded, taking a deep breath. "You're right. We can't give up now. There's got to be a way to crack this."

They spent the next few hours going over the evidence again, piece by piece. They reexamined witness statements, pored over crime scene photos, and reviewed the autopsy reports. But nothing new came to light. It was as if the killer had thought of everything, leaving no loose ends, no mistakes.

As the night wore on, Reynolds felt the weight of the case pressing down on him like never before. His eyes burned with fatigue, and his head throbbed with the effort of trying to make sense of the senseless. He could feel himself slipping, the obsessive need to solve the case gnawing away at his sanity.

At some point, Sarah must have noticed, because she gently suggested, "Maybe you should get some rest, Sheriff. You're no good to anyone if you're running on empty."

Reynolds shook his head. "I can't. I can't just walk away from this. Not when we're so close."

Sarah didn't argue, but the concern in her eyes deepened. She had seen this kind of obsession before in other detectives, and it never ended well. But she knew better than to push Reynolds when he was in this state. All she could do was be there for him and hope that they would catch a break before it was too late.

Finally, as dawn began to break outside the office windows, Reynolds let out a sigh and slumped back in his chair. "I don't know, Sarah. Maybe we're just not going to get this one."

Sarah gave him a sympathetic look. "We can't think like that. We've got to keep pushing, keep looking for that one clue that will tie it all together."

Reynolds nodded, though his heart wasn't in it. He was too tired, too worn down by the constant pressure, the endless questions with no answers. But he knew she was right. They couldn't stop now. Not when lives were on the line.

As the first rays of sunlight filtered through the blinds, casting long shadows across the room, Reynolds made a silent vow to himself. He would solve this case, no matter what it took. He would find the killer and bring them to justice. And maybe, just maybe, he would find some peace in the process.

But deep down, a nagging voice whispered that he might not survive the journey.

2

Echoes of the Past

Fifteen years had passed since the night that had forever changed the town of Millstone. The murder at the local 7-Eleven was still fresh in the minds of those who lived through it, a dark stain on the town's history that refused to fade.

It was a warm summer night when the crime took place. The 7-Eleven was one of the few places in town that stayed open late, a convenient stop for those who needed a last-minute gallon of milk or a pack of cigarettes. That night, however, it became the scene of a brutal murder that would haunt the town for years to come.

The victim, David Carmichael, was the night clerk, a quiet man in his mid-30s who kept to himself. He was found behind the counter, his body cold, a single gunshot wound to the chest. The cash register was empty, and there were no security cameras to capture what had happened. The only clue was a vague description from a witness—a bald, white male in his mid-20s, with a tattoo on his forearm, seen fleeing the scene on foot.

Detective James Reynolds had been on the force for only a few years when the case came across his desk. Millstone wasn't known for violent crime, and the murder shocked the community to its core. Reynolds was determined to bring the killer to justice, but the investigation quickly stalled. With no physical evidence and only the shaky testimony of a single witness, the case went cold.

But now, after all these years, a new lead had surfaced. Reynolds, older and more seasoned, sat in his office, the case file spread out before him. It had been years since he last looked at it, but every detail was etched in his memory. The door to his office opened, and Deputy Sarah Miller entered, her face serious.

"We've got a witness, Sheriff," Sarah said, holding up a file. "Someone who says they saw the guy who did it."

Reynolds looked up, his interest piqued. "After all this time? Who is it?"

"His name's Eddie Barker. Says he was living on the streets back then, didn't want to get involved at the time. But now... well, I guess he's had a change of heart."

Reynolds took the file and flipped through it. "What's he saying?"

"He says he saw a man matching the original description running out of the store that night. Bald, mid-20s, white male, with a tattoo on his right forearm. Barker's willing to testify."

Reynolds leaned back in his chair, the weight of the years heavy on his shoulders. "You think he's credible?"

Sarah hesitated. "Hard to say. He's got a bit of a record, but nothing violent. If he's telling the truth, this could be our guy."

Reynolds nodded slowly. "We'll bring him in, see if he can identify the suspect."

They worked quickly, tracing the suspect—Daniel Collins—who had been living in Millstone at the time of the murder. Daniel had left town shortly after the crime, but they found him living a quiet life in a neighboring city. He was now in his mid-30s, working as a mechanic, with no prior criminal record.

When Reynolds and Sarah arrived at Daniel's modest home, he answered the door with a wary look. "Can I help you?"

"Mr. Collins," Reynolds said, flashing his badge. "We're with the Millstone Police Department. We'd like to ask you a few questions about a case we're investigating."

Daniel's expression darkened, but he nodded. "Sure, come in."

They sat in Daniel's small living room, the walls adorned with pictures of classic cars and a few family photos. Daniel remained calm as Reynolds explained the reason for their visit, but there was a tension in the air that was impossible to ignore.

"So you're saying I'm a suspect in a murder that happened fifteen years ago?" Daniel asked, his voice measured.

"We're just following up on a lead," Reynolds replied. "A witness has come forward who says they saw you at the scene that night."

Daniel's jaw tightened. "I didn't kill anyone."

"Do you have an alibi for that night?" Sarah asked gently.

Daniel's eyes flickered with a hint of desperation. "I was at home. Alone. No one can vouch for me."

Reynolds nodded, his expression unreadable. "We'll need to take you down to the station for questioning. If you're innocent, this will all get sorted out."

Daniel's shoulders slumped as he stood. "I didn't do it," he repeated, more to himself than to them.

At the station, Daniel sat in the interrogation room, his hands resting on the table, his eyes fixed on the two-way mirror. Reynolds entered, followed by Sarah, and they took their seats across from him.

"Let's start from the beginning," Reynolds said, his tone even. "Tell us where you were that night."

Daniel sighed, running a hand over his bald head. "I already told you—I was at home. I'd just gotten off work. I didn't have a car, so I walked home, made dinner, and went to bed. That's it."

"And the tattoo?" Sarah asked, glancing at the inked pattern on his forearm.

Daniel looked down at his arm, a faint smile tugging at the corners of his mouth. "Got it when I was eighteen. Stupid decision, but it doesn't make me a killer."

Reynolds studied him, searching for any sign of deception. But Daniel's gaze was steady, his voice firm. Still, the circumstantial evidence was hard to ignore.

"We have a witness who's willing to testify that they saw you at the scene," Reynolds said. "If you're innocent, you need to help us prove it."

Daniel's eyes flashed with anger. "How am I supposed to do that? You're basing this whole thing on the word of one guy who didn't come forward until now? What if he's lying?"

Reynolds leaned forward, his voice low. "We're just trying to get to the truth. But you have to understand, the evidence we have doesn't look good for you."

Daniel's face paled as the weight of Reynolds' words sank in. "I didn't do it," he whispered.

The trial that followed was swift and unforgiving. The prosecution leaned heavily on the witness's testimony and the lack of an alibi. Despite Daniel's claims of innocence, the jury was swayed by the circumstantial evidence. In the end, he was convicted of the murder and sentenced to fifteen years in prison.

As Daniel was led away in handcuffs, Reynolds watched him go, a knot of unease tightening in his chest. He had done his job—he had followed the evidence and brought a killer to justice. But something about the case didn't sit right with him.

Years passed, and the murder at the 7-Eleven faded from memory, replaced by new cases and new challenges. But for Reynolds, the conviction of Daniel Collins remained a lingering doubt, a shadow that refused to fade. He had sent a man to prison, but in the quiet moments, when he was alone with his thoughts, he couldn't shake the feeling that he might have gotten it wrong.

3

The Final Move

The night was heavy with anticipation. Detective James Reynolds paced back and forth in the dim light of his office, his nerves on edge. Every detail of the grandmaster's analysis had been carefully considered, every potential move plotted out on the board. The weight of the situation pressed down on him, but he forced himself to stay focused.

His team had been deployed to the three locations Valery Ivanov had identified—the old mill by the river, the town square, and the abandoned train station. Each location was being watched with eagle eyes, every shadow monitored for movement. Reynolds had never felt the stakes so high. The killer had to be caught tonight; there was no other option.

As the hours dragged on, the tension in the air thickened. Reynolds could feel it in his chest, the tightness that came with the knowledge that something terrible was about to happen. His phone buzzed intermittently with updates from his team—nothing suspicious yet. The minutes turned into hours, the night slipping away as the waiting continued.

Reynolds checked his watch. 4:00 a.m. Dawn was only a couple of hours away, and still no sign of the killer. His frustration began to mount. Had they missed something? Was the killer playing them again, leading them into a trap of false expectations?

Deputy Sarah Miller's voice crackled over the radio. "Sheriff, we've been here for hours. Do you think he might have changed his plan?"

Reynolds paused, the question gnawing at him. "Stay sharp, Sarah," he replied, trying to mask his own doubt. "He's out there. We just need to be patient."

But even as he said it, doubt began to creep into his mind. What if they had been outmaneuvered again? The killer had proven to be unpredictable, always one step ahead. Reynolds felt the familiar knot of anxiety tighten in his gut. What if they had bet on the wrong moves?

He forced himself to stay calm, to keep believing that they were on the right track. But as the night dragged on with no sign of the killer, his confidence began to erode. The silence was deafening, the waiting unbearable.

Just as he was about to call it off, to tell his team to regroup, his phone rang. The sound was shrill, cutting through the quiet like a knife. "Reynolds," he answered, his voice tense.

The voice on the other end was frantic. "Sheriff, there's been another murder. It's... it's bad. You need to get to the scene right away."

Reynolds felt his heart drop. "Where?" he demanded, already grabbing his coat.

"It's... it's not at any of the locations we were watching," the voice stammered. "It's at the old chapel on the hill."

Reynolds' blood ran cold. The old chapel wasn't on Valery's list. It wasn't even close to the other locations. How had they missed this? How had the killer anticipated their every move and struck where they least expected?

He raced to the scene, his mind racing with a thousand thoughts. The drive felt interminable, every second ticking by like a hammer against his skull. He knew, deep down, that this was it. The killer had made his final move, and Reynolds had been checkmated.

When he arrived at the chapel, the scene was a nightmare. The early morning light cast long shadows across the grounds, the old stone building looming ominously in the distance. Police tape cordoned off the area, and officers moved about with grim expressions, their faces pale in the dawn light.

Reynolds pushed through the crowd, his heart pounding as he approached the entrance to the chapel. The air was thick with the smell of blood and decay, the scent of death hanging over the place like a shroud.

Inside, the scene was even worse. The victim—a young woman—was arranged on the cold stone floor in a grotesque parody of a chess piece. Her limbs were twisted in unnatural angles, her eyes staring blankly at the ceiling. And above her, scrawled in blood on the wall, was a single word: **"Checkmate."**

Reynolds stared at the word, his breath catching in his throat. The final move. The killer had outplayed him, had beaten him at his own game. He had known all along, had anticipated every step Reynolds would take, and had executed the final move with brutal precision.

But it was more than that. As Reynolds looked down at the victim, he realized with a sickening certainty that her position mirrored the final move of the championship game—the move that had won him the title all those years ago. The killer had not just beaten him; he had ended the game in a way that left no room for doubt. It was a final, devastating statement—one that told Reynolds he had been outclassed in every possible way.

Reynolds felt a wave of despair wash over him. He had lost. The killer had won, and there was nothing he could do to change that. He had been outsmarted, outmaneuvered, and now, as he stood there in the chapel, he knew that the game was over.

The drive back to the station was a blur. Reynolds barely registered the world around him, his mind consumed by the weight of his failure. When he finally walked through the doors of the station, the other officers looked at him with a mix of sympathy and confusion. They had expected him to return with a victory, to announce that the killer had been caught. But instead, he had come back empty-handed, defeated.

Reynolds didn't say a word as he walked to his office and closed the door behind him. He stood there for a long moment, staring at the chessboard on his desk. The pieces were still in place, frozen in mid-game, as if waiting for him to make the next move.

But there were no moves left to make.

Reynolds sank into his chair, the weight of his defeat pressing down on him like a physical burden. The killer had won, and he knew it. There was no coming back from this, no way to undo the damage that had been done.

The game was over.

And James Reynolds had lost.

4

The Quiet Victory

Daniel sat in the dimly lit living room of his modest apartment, the air thick with the rich scent of cigar smoke. The room was quiet, save for the soft crackling of the fire in the hearth and the occasional clink of the ice in his cocktail glass. Outside, the city was just beginning to wake up, the early morning light filtering through the curtains, casting long shadows across the floor.

He leaned back in his chair, savoring the moment, the taste of victory lingering on his tongue like the smoky burn of the whiskey. The chessboard on the table in front of him was a near-perfect replica of the one in Detective Reynolds' office. The pieces were arranged in the same positions, frozen in time at the exact moment when he had made the final move.

"Checkmate," he murmured to himself, a faint smile playing on his lips.

For years, Daniel had dreamed of this moment—of the day when he would finally outmaneuver the man who had destroyed his life. Reynolds had sent him to prison for a crime he hadn't committed, and in that cold, dark cell, Daniel had nurtured his anger, feeding it with every injustice, every moment of despair.

But anger alone wouldn't have been enough. Daniel was a chess player at heart, always thinking several moves ahead. He knew that if he was going to beat Reynolds, it would have to be on the detective's own turf—using the very skills that Reynolds had once prided himself on.

So he had planned, meticulously, patiently, waiting for the perfect moment to strike. And when that moment had come, he had played his moves flawlessly, leading Reynolds into a trap so elegant, so perfectly constructed, that the detective hadn't even realized he was being played until it was too late.

Now, sitting here in the quiet of his apartment, Daniel felt a strange sense of emptiness. He had won—he had defeated the man who had taken everything from him. But as he stared at the chessboard, the pieces locked in their final positions, he realized that victory wasn't as sweet as he had imagined it would be.

He had spent so long plotting his revenge, so long focused on the game, that now that it was over, he didn't know what to do next. The thrill of the chase, the satisfaction of outthinking his opponent—those were the things that had driven him, that had given his life meaning. But now that the game was finished, he was left with nothing but the hollow echo of his own triumph.

Daniel took a long drag on his cigar, letting the smoke curl up towards the ceiling. He could still see the look on Reynolds' face when he had found the final victim, the moment when he had realized that he had been beaten. It was a look of pure defeat, of a man who had finally been outmatched.

But instead of the satisfaction he had expected, Daniel felt a pang of something else—something that felt uncomfortably like guilt. He had become the very thing he had despised—a man willing to destroy others in the pursuit of his own ends.

The ice clinked in his glass as he took another sip, the warmth of the alcohol doing little to chase away the chill that had settled in his bones. He had won, yes. But at what cost? What did he have now, other than the knowledge that he had bested his enemy?

He was free, but in a way, he was still imprisoned—trapped in the memories of the life that had been stolen from him, and the life he had destroyed in return.

Daniel's eyes drifted to the window, where the first rays of the sun were breaking through the darkness. The new day brought with it the promise of a fresh start, but he couldn't shake the feeling that he was standing at the edge of something he didn't understand—something darker and more terrifying than anything he had faced before.

What did you do after you had won the game? What happened when there were no more moves to make?

The thought gnawed at him, and for the first time in years, Daniel felt truly lost.

He stubbed out his cigar in the ashtray, the glowing ember snuffed out with a hiss. The chessboard on the table seemed to mock him now, the pieces no longer symbols of victory, but of the emptiness that victory had brought.

Daniel stood up and walked to the window, looking out over the city that had been both his prison and his battleground. He had won, but in doing so, he had lost something far more important—his sense of purpose, his reason for playing the game in the first place.

With a sigh, he turned away from the window and headed towards the door. The apartment felt cold and lifeless, the silence oppressive. He didn't know where he was going, only that he couldn't stay here any longer.

As he stepped out into the cool morning air, Daniel knew that he had reached the end of one game. But he couldn't shake the feeling that another, far more dangerous game was just beginning—a game with no clear rules, no obvious opponents, and no guarantee of victory.

And this time, he wasn't sure if he was ready to play.

5

Shadows in the Night

The small town of Millstone was the kind of place where everyone knew each other by name. Tucked away from the bustle of the city, its charm lay in its simplicity—quiet streets lined with cozy homes, a main street with a handful of family-owned businesses, and a community that prided itself on its close-knit nature. For as long as anyone could remember, Millstone had been a sanctuary from the chaos of the world.

But that all changed one fateful night in early autumn.

It began innocuously enough. At first, people chalked up the disappearance of Betsy Thompson, a beloved elementary school teacher, to an unfortunate accident. Perhaps she had gotten lost on one of her evening walks through the woods, they said. Maybe she had decided to visit her sister in the next town without telling anyone. But when her body was found two days later, savagely murdered in a manner that defied explanation, the town's sense of security was shattered.

Sheriff Tom Harlow, a burly man in his mid-50s who had seen his fair share of accidents and domestic disputes but never a homicide, was the first to arrive at the scene. He crouched down beside Betsy's body, his brow furrowing as he examined the brutal wounds. There was no rhyme or reason to the attack—it was as if someone had unleashed their fury on her without warning or motive.

"What kind of monster could do this?" he muttered under his breath, more to himself than to his deputy, Sarah Miller, who stood nearby, her face pale.

Sarah swallowed hard, trying to keep her composure. "I don't know, Sheriff. I've never seen anything like this."

Tom stood up, his mind racing. "We need to lock this scene down, get the state police involved. This isn't something we can handle on our own."

Word of the murder spread through Millstone like wildfire. Within hours, the entire town was buzzing with rumors and speculation. At Joe's Diner, the usual morning crowd of farmers and retirees spoke in hushed tones, casting nervous glances at the door every time it swung open.

"Did you hear what happened to Betsy?" one of the regulars, an elderly man named Frank, whispered to his friend at the counter.

"Yeah, I heard," replied his friend, a wiry man named Bill. "Can't believe it. Who would do such a thing?"

Frank shook his head. "That's just it—no one knows. And from what I've heard, the police don't have any leads. It's like it happened out of nowhere."

At the local grocery store, the normally cheerful cashier, Linda, couldn't hide her unease as she rang up customers. "You be careful now," she said to each person as they left. "Keep an eye out, and don't go out alone after dark."

The fear was palpable, and it wasn't long before people started changing their routines. Parents who once let their children play outside until dusk now kept them indoors. The once lively streets of Millstone became eerily quiet as night fell, and the sense of unease hung in the air like a dense fog.

But the nightmare was only beginning.

A week after Betsy's murder, another body was found. This time, it was Jake Larson, the owner of the local hardware store. He had been well-liked, known for his warm smile and willingness to lend a hand to anyone in need. His death was as brutal as Betsy's, and once again, there were no clues—no signs of struggle, no fingerprints, nothing to point the police in the direction of the killer.

Sheriff Harlow was at a loss. "Two people dead in one week, and we've got nothing to go on," he said to Deputy Miller as they stood outside Jake's store, the flashing lights of the police cars illuminating the scene. "It doesn't make any sense."

Sarah nodded, her eyes scanning the growing crowd of onlookers. "Everyone's scared, Tom. They're starting to think we've got a serial killer on our hands."

Tom sighed heavily. "I know, and that's what worries me. Whoever's doing this... they're not leaving any trace. It's like they know exactly how to cover their tracks."

As the days passed, the fear in Millstone grew. People locked their doors and windows, installing security systems and buying weapons, something that had been virtually unheard of in the peaceful town. The local church held nightly prayer meetings, where residents gathered to seek comfort and protection. But even within those walls, the sense of dread was inescapable.

One evening, as the sun dipped below the horizon, Sheriff Harlow called an emergency town meeting at the community center. The large hall was packed with anxious faces, all of them looking to Tom for answers.

"Thank you all for coming," Tom began, his voice grave. "I know you're all scared, and I understand why. We've had two brutal murders in a short amount of time, and I wish I could stand here and tell you we have a suspect, but the truth is, we don't."

A murmur of concern rippled through the crowd.

"We've brought in the state police, and they're doing everything they can to help us," Tom continued. "But in the meantime, I need all of you to be vigilant. Don't take any unnecessary risks. If you see something suspicious, report it immediately."

A hand shot up from the back of the room. It belonged to Mary Jenkins, a local schoolteacher with a reputation for speaking her mind. "Sheriff, what are we supposed to do? We can't just stop living our lives."

Tom met her gaze. "I'm not asking you to stop living, Mary. But I am asking you to be cautious. Until we catch whoever's responsible, we all need to look out for each other."

After the meeting, Tom stood by the door, shaking hands with residents as they left. Many of them thanked him for his efforts, but he could see the fear in their eyes. It was a fear he shared—a fear that, no matter what they did, they were no closer to catching the killer.

That night, as Tom sat in his office, staring at the case files spread out before him, he couldn't shake the feeling that they were missing something. Something important. He replayed the details of the murders in his mind, searching for a connection, a pattern—anything that could give them a lead.

But the more he thought about it, the more elusive the answers seemed. The killings were random, senseless, and utterly terrifying. And as the clock ticked past midnight, Tom realized with a sinking feeling that the peace and safety of Millstone might be gone for good.

The next morning, Tom awoke to the sound of his phone ringing. He groggily answered, his heart skipping a beat when he heard the voice on the other end.

"Sheriff, it's happened again."

6

A King's Ascent

Daniel Porter was not born into a life of privilege. The streets of his neighborhood were rough, the kind where broken glass and discarded needles were as common as cracked sidewalks. The only constant in his life was the small apartment he shared with his mother, who worked two jobs just to keep the lights on. His father had left when Daniel was still in diapers, and he had never known anything else.

Growing up, Daniel learned quickly that life wasn't fair. At school, he was the quiet kid in the back of the classroom, often overlooked by teachers and peers alike. He didn't mind, though—he preferred it that way. It allowed him to watch, to observe, to think. He didn't have many friends, but he found solace in the school library, where he would spend hours devouring books on history, science, and eventually, chess.

It was by accident that Daniel discovered the game that would change his life. One rainy afternoon, when the other kids were running wild in the hallways, Daniel found an old chessboard tucked away on a dusty shelf in the library. Intrigued, he pulled it down and set it up on one of the tables. He didn't know the rules, but something about the pieces—the way they were arranged, the mystery of their movement—captivated him.

Mrs. Green, the school librarian, noticed Daniel's fascination. She was an older woman, with silver hair tied back in a neat bun and a pair of reading glasses that perched on the tip of her nose. She had seen many children come and go over the years, but there was something different about Daniel.

"Do you know how to play?" she asked, approaching the table with a kind smile.

Daniel shook his head. "No, ma'am. I've never played before."

Mrs. Green pulled out a chair and sat down across from him. "Well, you're in luck. Chess is a wonderful game, full of strategy and skill. Would you like to learn?"

Daniel's eyes lit up. "Yes, please."

Over the next few weeks, Mrs. Green taught Daniel the basics of the game. She explained the roles of each piece—the powerful queen, the steadfast rook, the cunning bishop. Daniel absorbed the information like a sponge, and it wasn't long before he was challenging her to games.

One afternoon, after yet another match in which Daniel had come close to winning, Mrs. Green leaned back in her chair, studying the boy across from her. "You have a real talent for this, Daniel. Have you ever thought about joining the school's chess club?"

Daniel hesitated. He had never considered himself particularly good at anything. But the idea of being part of something, of having a place where he belonged, was appealing. "Do you think I could?"

Mrs. Green smiled warmly. "I know you could. And I think you'd do very well."

Daniel took her advice and joined the chess club. At first, he was nervous. The other kids in the club had been playing for years, and he worried that he wouldn't measure up. But as the weeks went by, he began to realize that he had a natural gift for the game. He could see moves several steps ahead, anticipate his opponent's strategy, and adapt on the fly. His quiet determination and relentless focus quickly earned him the respect of his peers.

As Daniel grew older, his love for chess deepened. He entered local tournaments, where he often found himself facing off against players much older and more experienced than himself. But with each victory, his confidence grew. He studied the great masters—Bobby Fischer, Garry Kasparov, Anatoly Karpov—analyzing their games late into the night, his mind whirring with possibilities.

One evening, after a particularly grueling tournament, Daniel returned home to find his mother waiting for him in the small kitchen. She was a petite woman, worn thin by years of hard work, but her eyes sparkled with pride.

"How did it go?" she asked, setting a plate of leftovers in front of him.

Daniel shrugged, trying to play it cool, but he couldn't keep the excitement out of his voice. "I won."

His mother beamed. "That's my boy! I knew you could do it."

Daniel picked at his food, suddenly feeling a pang of guilt. "Mom, I know you're working really hard. I'm sorry I'm not helping more."

His mother reached across the table and took his hand. "Daniel, don't you worry about that. You're doing something amazing with this chess. You've got a real gift, and I want you to go as far as you can with it. Don't let anything hold you back, okay?"

Daniel nodded, though deep down, he knew the road ahead wouldn't be easy. But his mother's words gave him the strength to keep pushing forward.

As the years passed, Daniel's reputation as a chess prodigy spread. He began competing in state tournaments, then regional ones. Each time, the competition grew fiercer, but Daniel rose to the challenge, his skill and determination unmatched.

It wasn't long before he caught the attention of national chess organizations. Offers for sponsorships and invitations to prestigious tournaments started pouring in. For the first time in his life, Daniel felt like he was truly on the path to something great.

His big break came when he was invited to compete in the National Chess Championship. It was the culmination of everything he had worked for, and the pressure was immense. But Daniel was undeterred. He knew that this was his moment, and he was ready.

The championship was held in a grand hall in New York City, a far cry from the quiet streets of his hometown. The room was filled with the best players in the country, and the atmosphere was electric. Daniel felt a surge of adrenaline as he took his seat at the board, his opponent, a seasoned grandmaster, sitting across from him.

The match was intense, with each player pushing the other to their limits. The crowd watched in rapt silence as the pieces moved across the board, the tension in the room palpable. Daniel's mind raced as he calculated his next move, his heart pounding in his chest.

Finally, after what felt like an eternity, Daniel saw his opening. He moved his queen into position, setting up a checkmate that his opponent couldn't escape. The crowd erupted in applause as the grandmaster conceded defeat, a look of respect in his eyes.

As Daniel stood to accept his trophy, he felt a wave of emotions wash over him. He had done it—he was the national chess champion. All the years of hard work, of sacrifice, had paid off.

7

Clues in the Dark

Detective James Reynolds was not a man easily shaken. He had seen his share of gruesome crime scenes and faced down dangerous criminals in his twenty-five years on the force. But the recent string of murders in Millstone had him on edge in a way he hadn't felt since his early days as a rookie detective.

It wasn't just the brutality of the killings—it was the lack of anything that made sense. Each crime scene seemed to defy logic, as if the killer was playing a twisted game, leaving no trace behind, no evidence to follow. It was as if the killer was a ghost, slipping in and out of the night without a sound.

Reynolds sat at his desk in the small, cluttered office of the Millstone Police Department, staring at the photos pinned to the corkboard in front of him. Each image showed the face of a victim, eyes forever closed, lives violently cut short. Betsy Thompson, Jake Larson, and three others—each murder more senseless and horrifying than the last.

Sarah Miller, his loyal deputy, entered the room, a file in her hand. "Got the coroner's report on the latest victim, Sheriff. Nothing new—no signs of struggle, no defensive wounds, and no DNA other than the victim's."

Reynolds let out a heavy sigh, rubbing his temples. "That makes five, Sarah. Five people dead, and we're no closer to catching this bastard than we were after the first one."

Sarah sat down across from him, her expression one of concern. "What do we do now, Sheriff? We've interviewed everyone in town, gone through every piece of evidence, and still nothing. It's like this guy doesn't exist."

Reynolds leaned back in his chair, staring up at the ceiling as if the answers might be hiding in the old water stains above. "We're missing something, Sarah. Something obvious. No one can pull this off without leaving something behind. It's just... there's nothing connecting these people. They didn't know each other, didn't run in the same circles... hell, some of them barely left their homes."

Sarah frowned, flipping through the pages of the report. "I've been thinking about that too. What if it's not about the victims at all? What if it's about the locations?"

Reynolds sat up, intrigued. "Go on."

"Well," Sarah continued, "I've been looking at where the bodies were found. They're all over town, sure, but maybe there's a pattern we're not seeing. Something that ties these places together—maybe the killer's trying to send a message."

Reynolds nodded, his mind racing. "Get me a map, Sarah. Let's see if we can figure this out."

Sarah quickly grabbed a large map of Millstone from the filing cabinet and spread it out on Reynolds' desk. Together, they marked the locations of each murder with red push pins.

"Now, let's think," Reynolds said, more to himself than to Sarah. "If this guy is smart—and I think he is—then he's not just picking these places at random. There's got to be something tying them together."

They stared at the map in silence for a long moment. The pins seemed to mock them, like the scattered pieces of a puzzle that refused to fit.

"I don't see it," Sarah admitted, frustration creeping into her voice.

"Neither do I," Reynolds replied, his voice grim. "But we're not going to give up. We're going to keep looking until we find something—anything—that gives us a lead."

The hours passed as they pored over the map and files, searching for any clue, no matter how small. But as the night wore on, the weight of the case began to press down on Reynolds. His eyes burned from lack of sleep, and the nagging feeling that he was missing something crucial gnawed at him.

Finally, Sarah spoke up, her voice hesitant. "Sheriff... maybe it's time to call in some outside help. We've been at this for weeks, and we're getting nowhere. Maybe someone with fresh eyes could see something we're not."

Reynolds considered her suggestion, his pride warring with the growing sense of desperation. He had always prided himself on being able to solve even the most difficult cases, but this one... this one was different.

"Maybe you're right," he said quietly. "I'll make the call in the morning."

But as the words left his mouth, the phone on his desk rang, startling both of them. Reynolds answered it, his hand trembling slightly. It was the dispatcher.

"Sheriff, we just got a call. There's been another murder."

Reynolds felt his stomach drop. "Where?"

"Out on Old Mill Road, near the river. It's bad, Sheriff. Real bad."

Reynolds hung up without another word, grabbing his coat as he rushed out the door. Sarah was right behind him, the sound of their footsteps echoing down the empty hallway.

The drive to the crime scene was silent, the only sound the hum of the engine and the occasional crackle of the radio. When they arrived, the scene was already crawling with officers, their faces pale and drawn.

Reynolds approached the body, his heart pounding in his chest. The victim was a young woman, her lifeless eyes staring up at the night sky. The brutality of the attack was shocking, even after everything Reynolds had seen.

"Jesus," Sarah whispered, her hand covering her mouth.

Reynolds knelt beside the body, his eyes scanning the area for any sign of the killer. But there was nothing—no footprints, no broken branches, no discarded weapon. It was as if the killer had vanished into thin air.

He stood up, his hands clenched into fists. "This has to end," he said, his voice tight with barely controlled rage. "We're going to find this son of a bitch if it's the last thing we do."

But as the night wore on and the scene was processed, Reynolds couldn't shake the feeling that they were dealing with something far more sinister than a run-of-the-mill killer. Whoever was behind these murders was playing a game—one that Reynolds feared he might not be able to win.

Back at the station, Reynolds and Sarah sat in the dim light of the office, the map of Millstone still spread out before them. The weight of the unsolved murders hung heavy in the air, and the silence between them was thick with frustration.

"What do we do now?" Sarah asked quietly.

Reynolds stared at the map, the lines and pins blurring together in his tired eyes. "We keep going," he said, his voice filled with determination. "We keep looking until we find the clue that breaks this case wide open."

But as the days turned into weeks and the killer remained elusive, Reynolds found himself slipping further into obsession. The case consumed him, the faces of the victims haunting his every waking moment. He began to doubt himself, to question whether he was still capable of solving the case.

He spent long nights alone in his office, the walls closing in around him as he stared at the evidence, trying to make sense of it all. His health began to suffer—his eyes were bloodshot, his hands trembled with fatigue, and the dark circles under his eyes deepened with each passing day.

Sarah watched with growing concern as Reynolds pushed himself to the brink, but she knew better than to confront him. He was a man on a mission, driven by a need to catch the killer before anyone else was hurt. But she feared that if they didn't get a break soon, Reynolds might not survive the case.

The town of Millstone remained gripped by fear, the once-bustling streets now deserted as night fell. People locked their doors and windows, afraid to step outside after dark. The killer had turned their quiet town into a place of nightmares, and no one knew when—or if—it would end.

Reynolds knew that time was running out. Each day that passed brought the killer closer to his next victim, and each night that Reynolds spent staring at the map, searching for a pattern that wasn't there, brought him closer to the edge.

But he refused to give up. He couldn't. The lives of the people in Millstone depended on him, and he would do whatever it took to bring the killer to justice.

Even if it meant losing himself in the process.

8

The New Player

It was a crisp autumn evening when the stranger first walked into the Millstone Chess Club. The club met in a modest room above the town's library, where the wooden floors creaked with age and the scent of old books lingered in the air. The small group of regulars, mostly retirees and a few younger enthusiasts, had just finished setting up their boards when the door opened, drawing their attention.

The man who entered was in his mid-thirties, with a lean build and a quiet demeanor. He wore a worn leather jacket, and his short hair was neatly combed. There was something unassuming about him, the kind of person who could easily blend into a crowd. But as he stepped further into the room, the players couldn't help but notice his sharp eyes, which seemed to take in every detail.

"Hello there," greeted Mr. Thompson, the club's de facto leader, a retired schoolteacher with a passion for chess. "Looking to join the game?"

The stranger offered a polite smile and nodded. "If you don't mind. I'm new in town and thought I'd see if there were any chess players around."

"Well, you've come to the right place," Mr. Thompson replied warmly. "We're always happy to have new members. What's your name, son?"

"Ethan," the man said simply. "Ethan Gray."

"Welcome, Ethan," Mr. Thompson said, motioning for him to take a seat. "Why don't you join us for a game?"

Ethan sat down at one of the boards, opposite a young man named Daniel, who had been the club's unofficial champion for a few years.

Daniel was a skilled player, confident in his abilities, and he eyed Ethan with a mixture of curiosity and competitive spirit.

"Ready when you are," Daniel said, giving Ethan a nod.

Ethan returned the nod and made the first move. The game began quietly, the room filled with the soft clicks of pieces being moved across the boards. The other players occasionally glanced over, intrigued by the newcomer's style of play.

It didn't take long for them to realize that Ethan was good—very good. His moves were precise, his strategy methodical. But he wasn't unbeatable. Daniel managed to hold his own, and after a tense forty minutes, the game ended in a draw.

"Well played," Daniel said, offering his hand across the board.

Ethan shook it with a small smile. "You too. It's been a while since I had a game like that."

Mr. Thompson, who had been watching the match closely, clapped his hands together. "Well, Ethan, I think you'll fit right in here. It's not often we get someone who can give Daniel a run for his money."

Ethan chuckled softly. "I just enjoy the game. It's nice to find a place where people take it seriously."

As the evening went on, Ethan played a few more games, chatting casually with the other members between matches. He was friendly, but reserved, offering little about himself beyond the basics. He mentioned that he had recently moved to Millstone, looking for a fresh start, and that he had taken a job at a local car repair shop. The members of the club were welcoming, happy to have someone new to play against, and didn't press him for details.

Over the next few weeks, Ethan became a regular fixture at the club. He showed up every Thursday evening, always punctual, always ready for a game. He quickly became well-liked by the other members, who appreciated his skill and quiet demeanor. He never boasted about his victories, nor did he sulk when he lost. He was, in every sense, a model player.

But as time went on, some of the club members began to notice little things about Ethan that seemed... off. It wasn't anything they could put their finger on, just a feeling—a certain coldness in his eyes when he focused on the board, a slight tension in his posture when he was deep in thought. It was as if, beneath the calm exterior, there was something else—something darker.

One evening, after the games had wrapped up and most of the members had gone home, Mr. Thompson found himself alone with Ethan, packing up the boards. They worked in comfortable silence for a few minutes before Mr. Thompson spoke up.

"You know, Ethan," he began, choosing his words carefully, "you're quite the player. I've been around chess long enough to recognize real talent when I see it. Have you ever thought about playing in tournaments?"

Ethan glanced up, a faint smile on his lips. "I've played in a few over the years. But I'm not really interested in the competition anymore. I play for the love of the game."

Mr. Thompson nodded, but he couldn't shake the feeling that there was more to it than that. "Where did you play before you came to Millstone?"

Ethan paused, as if considering how to answer. "Here and there. I've moved around a lot. I guess you could say I'm a bit of a drifter."

"I see," Mr. Thompson said, though he didn't quite believe it. "Well, we're glad to have you here. It's always good to have someone who can challenge the rest of us."

Ethan's smile didn't reach his eyes. "I'm glad to be here too."

As the months passed, Ethan's presence in the club became a given, something the members looked forward to each week. But outside the club, he remained something of an enigma. He was polite and cordial when he interacted with people around town, but he kept to himself, never revealing much about his past or his personal life.

He rented a small apartment on the edge of town, near the repair shop where he worked. The owner of the shop, a grizzled old mechanic named Frank, had taken a liking to Ethan, appreciating his work ethic and skill with cars. But even Frank, who had seen all kinds of people come and go over the years, couldn't help but feel that there was something about Ethan that didn't quite add up.

One day, as they were closing up the shop, Frank decided to ask him about it.

"You don't talk much about yourself, Ethan," Frank said, wiping his hands on a rag. "Not that it's any of my business, but a man's got to have a story. What's yours?"

Ethan shrugged, a distant look in his eyes. "Not much to tell. I've had a few rough patches, but who hasn't? Just trying to make a new start here."

Frank nodded slowly. "Well, you're doing good work. You're welcome to stay as long as you need."

"Thanks, Frank," Ethan replied, though his tone was flat. "I appreciate it."

As Frank watched him leave, a nagging feeling tugged at the back of his mind. Ethan was a good worker, no doubt about that. But there was something else there—something he couldn't quite place. It was almost as if Ethan was hiding something, though what it could be, Frank had no idea.

Over time, Ethan's quiet presence began to weave itself into the fabric of the town. People knew him as the guy who worked at Frank's shop, the man who played chess at the club, the new face in a small community where everyone knew everyone else. But no one really knew him. And as the days turned into months, his presence in the town's past began to take on a more ominous significance.

The chess club continued to meet every Thursday, and Ethan continued to play, his skills honed with each passing game. But Mr. Thompson couldn't shake the feeling that there was more to Ethan than met the eye. He watched him closely, noting the way Ethan seemed to study his opponents, the way he seemed to anticipate their moves before they even made them. It was as if Ethan was playing a different game, one that only he understood.

And then there were the nights when Ethan would disappear for hours at a time, no one knowing where he had gone or what he was doing. When asked, he would simply shrug and say he liked to take long walks, to clear his head. But the truth was, no one really knew where he went, and no one dared to ask too many questions.

As Ethan became more entrenched in the community, his presence began to take on a more sinister tone. People started to whisper, to wonder about the man who had come to their town with no past, no story. What was he hiding? And why had he really come to Millstone?

The answers, it seemed, were hidden beneath the surface, waiting to be uncovered. But for now, Ethan remained an enigma, a mystery that no one could solve.

And as the shadows grew longer in the town of Millstone, so too did the unease that settled over its residents, like a dark cloud gathering on the horizon.

9

The Pattern Beneath

Detective James Reynolds stood in his office, staring intently at the large corkboard that had become the focal point of his life over the past few months. The board was cluttered with maps, photos, and notes, all connected by a web of red string. Each string represented a possible connection between the murders that had plagued Millstone, each note a potential clue that could unravel the mystery.

Reynolds had been working tirelessly, barely sleeping, driven by the need to find a pattern in the chaos. He was certain that if he could just figure out the killer's logic, he could predict the next move and stop the murders once and for all. The pressure to solve the case weighed heavily on him, pushing him to the brink of obsession.

Sarah Miller, his trusted deputy, entered the room carrying two cups of coffee. She paused in the doorway, watching Reynolds with a mixture of concern and admiration. He was a good detective—one of the best—but this case was taking a toll on him. His usually sharp features were drawn, his eyes bloodshot from lack of sleep.

"Sheriff," Sarah called gently, holding out one of the cups. "You need to take a break. You've been at this for hours."

Reynolds barely glanced at her, his mind too engrossed in the web of information in front of him. "I'm close, Sarah. I can feel it. There's a pattern here, I just need to find it."

Sarah sighed and stepped closer, placing the coffee on his desk. "You said that last week, and the week before that. Maybe it's time to step back, look at this with fresh eyes."

Reynolds finally turned to face her, his expression one of grim determination. "I don't have time to step back. Every minute I waste is another minute the killer is out there, planning his next move."

Sarah shook her head, concern deepening the lines on her face. "But if you burn yourself out, Sheriff, you won't be any good to anyone."

Reynolds clenched his jaw, frustration bubbling beneath the surface. He knew she was right, but he couldn't afford to stop now. Not when he was so close. "I appreciate your concern, Sarah, but I need to see this through."

Sarah hesitated, then nodded. She had worked with Reynolds long enough to know when to back off. "Just... promise me you'll take care of yourself. We need you."

Reynolds gave her a small, tight smile. "I will, Sarah. I promise."

With that, Sarah left the room, closing the door softly behind her. Reynolds turned back to the board, his mind racing. He replayed the details of each murder in his head, trying to find the common thread that connected them. His eyes darted from one location on the map to another, each marked with a red pin.

Suddenly, something clicked. His heart began to race as he realized there was a pattern—a sequence in the dates and locations. It wasn't immediately obvious, but when he plotted the murders on a calendar and overlaid them with the map, he saw it: a rough, yet discernible pattern.

He quickly grabbed a marker and began circling the dates and locations, connecting them with lines. The more he worked, the clearer the pattern became. It was almost as if the killer was moving in a calculated, methodical way—following a twisted schedule.

Reynolds stepped back and stared at the board, his heart pounding in his chest. He had done it. He had found the pattern. And with it, he believed he could predict where and when the next murder would happen.

He hurriedly called Sarah back into the room. "Sarah, I've got it," he said, his voice filled with a mix of excitement and urgency. "I know where the next murder is going to happen."

Sarah looked at the board, her eyes widening as she followed the lines and circles Reynolds had drawn. "Are you sure?"

Reynolds nodded, his confidence returning. "I'm sure. It's going to happen at the old warehouse on 3rd Street, three days from now. The timing fits perfectly with the pattern."

Sarah's face mirrored his determination. "Then we need to act fast. We'll set up surveillance and catch this guy before he can strike again."

For the first time in weeks, Reynolds felt a glimmer of hope. This was their chance to stop the killer, to end the nightmare that had gripped Millstone. They quickly put a plan into action, coordinating with the rest of the police department to cover all exits of the warehouse.

As the day of the predicted murder approached, the tension in the department was palpable. Reynolds barely slept, spending most of his time at the station, double and triple-checking his calculations. The thought of something going wrong gnawed at him, but he pushed it aside, focusing on the task at hand.

The night of the stakeout, Reynolds and Sarah sat in an unmarked car across from the warehouse, watching the dark, looming structure with steely determination. The rest of the team was in position, ready to move at a moment's notice.

Hours passed in silence, the only sounds the occasional rustle of leaves in the wind and the distant hum of traffic. Every now and then, Reynolds would glance at his watch, counting down the minutes until the expected time of the attack.

But as the clock ticked past midnight, a sense of unease began to creep into Reynolds' mind. The warehouse remained dark and silent, no sign of the killer or any activity. His confidence started to waver, doubt creeping in like a cold chill.

"What if we're wrong?" Sarah whispered, breaking the silence.

Reynolds clenched his fists, his jaw tight. "We're not wrong. The pattern... it has to be right."

But as the hours dragged on with no sign of the killer, Reynolds felt his hope slipping away. By dawn, it was clear that nothing was going to happen. The killer had outsmarted them, had somehow known they were waiting.

Reynolds' heart sank as he realized the gravity of the situation. His theory—his carefully calculated pattern—had been wrong. And now, the killer was still out there, free to strike again.

When they returned to the station, the sense of failure was heavy in the air. Reynolds retreated to his office, closing the door behind him. He sank into his chair, staring blankly at the board that had once seemed so promising. Now, it felt like a cruel joke, a mockery of his efforts.

Sarah knocked softly before entering. She saw the look of defeat on Reynolds' face and felt a pang of sympathy. "Sheriff, it's not your fault. We did everything we could."

Reynolds shook his head, his voice hollow. "But it wasn't enough. I failed. I let everyone down."

Sarah stepped closer, her voice gentle but firm. "You didn't fail. This isn't over. We'll figure it out. We just need to keep going."

But Reynolds couldn't shake the feeling of despair that had taken hold of him. He had been so sure, so confident that he had cracked the code. And yet, he had been wrong. The self-doubt gnawed at him, making him question his instincts, his abilities.

As Sarah left him alone with his thoughts, Reynolds stared at the board, the lines and pins blurring together in his tired eyes. The sense of control he had felt was gone, replaced by a crushing weight of uncertainty. And in that moment, he realized just how close he was to losing himself in the darkness that had claimed so many lives.

10

Descent into Darkness

Detective James Reynolds had always prided himself on his ability to stay calm under pressure, to keep a clear head when others faltered. But the last few months had pushed him to his limits, and he was beginning to unravel.

The failure of his carefully calculated prediction had been a crushing blow. For days, he couldn't shake the sense of defeat, the gnawing fear that he might never solve the case. The confidence that had once driven him was now eroded, replaced by a growing doubt that gnawed at his every thought.

Reynolds' office had become a prison. He spent most of his time there, poring over the same evidence again and again, as if hoping that the answers would magically appear. The corkboard that had once seemed like the key to solving the case now mocked him with its tangled web of red string and cryptic notes.

The sleepless nights began to take their toll. Reynolds' once sharp eyes were now dull and bloodshot, the bags under them growing darker with each passing day. He found it harder and harder to focus, his thoughts clouded by exhaustion and frustration.

It wasn't long before he turned to alcohol for solace. At first, it was just a drink or two in the evenings, something to take the edge off. But soon, the drinks became more frequent, and the nights longer. The whiskey burned as it went down, but it numbed the pain, at least for a little while.

One evening, as Reynolds sat slumped in his office chair, a half-empty bottle of whiskey on his desk, Sarah Miller knocked on the door. When he didn't respond, she opened it gently and stepped inside. The sight of her boss—the man she had always looked up to—broke her heart.

"Sheriff," she said softly, her voice laced with concern. "You need to stop this. You're killing yourself."

Reynolds looked up at her, his eyes bleary. "What's the point, Sarah? I can't do it. I can't solve this damn case. I'm a failure."

Sarah shook her head, stepping closer. "You're not a failure, James. You're just human. You're doing everything you can, but you can't do it alone."

Reynolds snorted, the sound bitter and humorless. "I've always done it alone. That's how I've always worked. But now... now I don't even know if I can trust my own instincts."

Sarah reached out and placed a hand on his shoulder. "You don't have to do it alone. Let us help you. We're a team, remember?"

Reynolds sighed, the weight of the world pressing down on him. "I don't know how much more I can take, Sarah. I'm tired. I'm so damn tired."

"Then take a break," she urged. "Get some rest. Let us handle things for a while. You need to take care of yourself."

Reynolds shook his head stubbornly. "I can't. I can't just walk away from this. If I do, then the killer wins."

"You won't be walking away," Sarah insisted. "You'll be taking a step back so you can come back stronger. You're no good to anyone like this, James."

But Reynolds wasn't listening. He pushed the bottle of whiskey aside and buried his face in his hands, his shoulders slumping in defeat. "I've lost it, Sarah. I've lost whatever it was that made me a good detective."

Sarah's heart ached for him, but she knew there was only so much she could do. She had seen this kind of burnout before, and it never ended well. But she couldn't force him to take care of himself. All she could do was be there for him, to offer her support and hope that he would accept it.

As the days turned into weeks, Reynolds became more and more isolated. He stopped talking to his colleagues, stopped returning phone calls. He avoided his friends, no longer able to face their concerned questions. The only thing that mattered to him was the case—the case that had become his obsession, his torment.

His drinking grew worse. He would stumble into the station in the early hours of the morning, reeking of alcohol, his hands shaking as he tried to focus on the paperwork that piled up on his desk. His once pristine appearance was now disheveled, his clothes rumpled, his hair unkempt. The man who had once been the pride of the Millstone Police Department was now a shadow of his former self.

One night, after the rest of the station had gone home, Reynolds sat alone in his office, the dim light from his desk lamp casting long shadows across the room. The whiskey bottle was empty, lying on its side on the desk, and Reynolds stared blankly at the corkboard, his vision swimming.

He could feel himself slipping, could feel the darkness closing in around him. But he didn't have the strength to fight it anymore. The pressure, the constant stress—it was all too much.

His thoughts were a jumbled mess, a chaotic tangle of fear, anger, and despair. He could hear the voices of the victims, their cries for justice echoing in his mind, taunting him, accusing him of failing them. He slammed his fists on the desk, a raw scream of frustration tearing from his throat.

"Why can't I do this?" he shouted to the empty room. "Why can't I figure it out?"

But there was no answer. There was only silence, heavy and oppressive, suffocating him. He buried his face in his hands, the weight of his failure crushing him.

The hours dragged on, and eventually, Reynolds passed out at his desk, the alcohol and exhaustion finally overtaking him. But even in sleep, there was no peace. His dreams were filled with images of the murders, the blood, the horror, and the relentless guilt that gnawed at him.

When he awoke the next morning, his head pounding and his mouth dry, he knew he was reaching his breaking point. But the thought of giving up, of walking away from the case, was unbearable. He had to solve it. He had to. But deep down, he feared that he might never find the answers he so desperately sought.

As Reynolds stared at the corkboard, the tangled web of string and notes mocking him, he realized that he was caught in a trap of his own making. The case had become his obsession, his life, and it was slowly destroying him.

And he didn't know how to stop it.

11

The Red Queen's Gambit

It was late in the afternoon when Detective James Reynolds received the call. The sun was beginning to set, casting long shadows across the empty streets of Millstone. The voice on the other end of the line was that of a concerned citizen, a woman who had noticed strange activity at an old, abandoned house on the outskirts of town. She mentioned seeing someone going in and out of the house at odd hours, and while she couldn't see much, she had an uneasy feeling about it.

Reynolds listened intently, his senses sharpening despite the fog of exhaustion that had clouded his mind for weeks. The case had been at a standstill, with no new leads, no fresh clues. The prospect of something—anything—that might bring him closer to solving the murders was enough to get him moving.

"I'll check it out," Reynolds said, jotting down the address the woman gave him. "Thank you for calling."

He hung up the phone and grabbed his coat, the familiar weight of his gun pressing against his side as he holstered it. The walk to his car was brisk, his mind racing with possibilities. An abandoned house, strange activity—it could be nothing, or it could be the break he'd been waiting for.

As he drove through the quiet streets, Reynolds couldn't help but feel a sense of déjà vu. The house was on the outskirts of town, a place where few people ventured unless they had a reason. It had once been a grand home, but years of neglect had taken their toll. The windows were boarded up, the yard overgrown with weeds. The place had an air of desolation about it, a forgotten relic of a time long past.

Reynolds parked his car a little ways down the road and approached the house on foot. The crunch of gravel under his shoes was the only sound in the stillness of the evening. He reached the front door, which hung slightly ajar, and pushed it open with a creak.

The air inside was stale, thick with the smell of dust and decay. Reynolds stepped cautiously into the entryway, his hand instinctively going to his gun. The floorboards groaned under his weight as he moved deeper into the house, the dim light from outside barely penetrating the gloom.

He made his way through the rooms, each one more dilapidated than the last. Peeling wallpaper, broken furniture, and debris littered the floors. But it was in the living room that Reynolds found something that made him stop in his tracks.

The walls were covered in strange markings—intricate patterns that, at first glance, seemed chaotic. But as Reynolds looked closer, he realized they were not random at all. They were chess positions, carefully drawn in what appeared to be blood. He reached out, touching the marks with his fingers, and brought them close to his nose. The scent was unmistakable: paint, not blood.

He exhaled a breath he hadn't realized he was holding, a mixture of relief and confusion washing over him. Who would go to the trouble of painting chess moves on the walls of an abandoned house? And why?

As he examined the positions more closely, Reynolds noticed something unsettling. The moves weren't just random—they were specific sequences from famous games, ones he recognized from his years as a competitive chess player. His pulse quickened as he realized that whoever had done this knew exactly what they were doing. This wasn't the work of a vandal or a squatter. This was deliberate, methodical.

Reynolds moved from room to room, each wall telling a different part of the story. The positions seemed to flow from one room to the next, as if the house itself was a chessboard, each move leading inevitably to the next.

In the final room, what appeared to be the endgame was painted on the wall in large, sweeping strokes. The red paint dripped down like blood, giving the impression of violence, of something dark and sinister. Reynolds stood in front of it, his mind racing.

What did it mean? Was this some kind of message? A warning? Or was it something more personal—something aimed directly at him?

He pulled out his phone and took pictures of the walls, documenting every position, every detail. He would need time to analyze this, to figure out what the killer was trying to convey. But as he stood there, staring at the final move on the wall, a sense of dread settled in his gut.

The absence of any other evidence in the house was both frustrating and alarming. There were no fingerprints, no footprints, no signs of who had been there or why. It was as if the person responsible had vanished into thin air, leaving behind only this eerie, cryptic message.

Reynolds left the house with more questions than answers. The drive back to the station was a blur, his mind consumed with thoughts of the chess positions, of the strange, unsettling feeling that this house held a key to the mystery, even if it wasn't immediately clear what that key was.

Back at the station, he spread the photos out on his desk, studying them intently. The positions, the moves—they were familiar, but there was something off about them. Something he couldn't quite put his finger on.

Sarah Miller knocked on the doorframe before stepping into the office. "Sheriff, you okay?"

Reynolds looked up, his eyes dark with thought. "I found something. In an abandoned house on the outskirts of town. Chess positions, painted on the walls in red."

Sarah frowned, intrigued. "Chess positions? What do you think it means?"

"I don't know yet," Reynolds admitted. "But it's deliberate. The moves—they're from famous games. Whoever did this knows their chess."

Sarah studied the photos with him, the two of them falling into a contemplative silence. Finally, she spoke. "It's strange, isn't it? Why would someone go through all this trouble? What are they trying to tell us?"

Reynolds shook his head. "That's what I need to figure out. I just... I can't shake the feeling that this house is important. That there's something there, something we're missing."

Sarah nodded, her expression serious. "Maybe it's a clue. Or maybe it's a trap."

Reynolds looked at the final position, the one that seemed to scream out at him from the wall. "Either way, it's all we've got."

He knew that the discovery at the abandoned house was far from the end of the case. If anything, it was just the beginning of a new chapter, one that promised to be even more dangerous and disturbing than what had come before.

As he sat back in his chair, exhaustion tugging at the edges of his mind, Reynolds couldn't shake the feeling that the chessboard had been set, and the pieces were already in motion. The next move would be crucial—both for him and for the killer.

And this time, there was no room for error.

12

Game of Shadows

Detective James Reynolds couldn't escape the images that haunted his mind. The chess positions, painted in stark red on the walls of the abandoned house, had lodged themselves in his thoughts like a splinter he couldn't remove. No matter how hard he tried to push them aside, they kept resurfacing, gnawing at him with their eerie familiarity.

It had been days since his first visit to the house, but the strange discovery lingered with him. There was something about those positions—something he felt he should understand, but couldn't quite grasp. The sense of unease gnawed at him, keeping him awake at night, his thoughts churning restlessly.

Finally, unable to ignore the pull any longer, Reynolds decided to return to the house. He had to see the positions again, to study them more closely. Perhaps there was something he had missed, some detail that would finally bring clarity to the murky thoughts swirling in his mind.

He arrived at the house just as the sun was beginning to set, casting long shadows across the overgrown yard. The house loomed before him, a decrepit relic of a forgotten past. Reynolds took a deep breath and stepped inside, the familiar smell of dust and decay greeting him like an old acquaintance.

The living room was exactly as he had left it, the chess positions still stark against the peeling wallpaper. Reynolds moved from wall to wall, his eyes scanning the painted moves, his mind working furiously to make sense of them.

But despite his efforts, nothing came to him. The positions seemed random, disconnected from any game he could recall. Frustration bubbled up inside him, and he clenched his fists, resisting the urge to lash out at the walls.

"This doesn't make any sense," he muttered to himself, his voice echoing in the empty room.

He pulled out his phone and began taking photographs of the positions, capturing every angle, every detail. If he couldn't figure it out now, perhaps he could at home, in the quiet of his office, where he could study the images without the oppressive atmosphere of the house pressing down on him.

As he snapped the final photo, Reynolds paused, his gaze lingering on the endgame position painted in bold, sweeping strokes. There was something about it that tugged at his memory, something that felt both familiar and alien at the same time. But try as he might, he couldn't place it.

With a sigh, Reynolds left the house and drove home, the weight of the mystery pressing down on him. He needed answers, but they seemed just out of reach, like a word on the tip of his tongue that refused to be spoken.

That night, he sat in his dimly lit office, the photographs spread out before him. The walls of his office were still cluttered with the remnants of the investigation—maps, crime scene photos, and red string connecting various points of interest. But now, those seemed distant, secondary to the enigma laid out on his desk.

Reynolds leaned back in his chair, his eyes narrowing as he studied the images. His mind drifted back to his younger years, to the days when chess had been his passion, his escape from the world. He had spent countless hours poring over books of famous games, memorizing the strategies of the great masters. He had even competed in national tournaments, rising through the ranks to become a champion.

But that was a lifetime ago, before the weight of the world had settled on his shoulders, before the burdens of his job had consumed him. He had long since put those days behind him, trading the chessboard for the badge, the quiet contemplation of the game for the chaos of the real world.

Yet now, as he stared at the positions on the walls, the memories came flooding back. He could almost feel the cool, smooth surface of the chess pieces in his hands, the thrill of anticipating his opponent's next move, the satisfaction of executing a flawless strategy.

And then, like a bolt of lightning, it hit him.

Reynolds sat up straight, his heart pounding in his chest. The positions—they weren't random. They were deliberate, calculated. Each one was part of a larger sequence, a sequence that he knew all too well.

He grabbed a notebook and began scribbling down the moves, his mind racing as he tried to reconstruct the game from memory. The more he wrote, the more certain he became. This wasn't just any game. It was one of his own, a game he had played years ago, in the finals of the national championship.

His opponent had been a formidable player, pushing him to the brink in a match that had lasted hours. But in the end, Reynolds had emerged victorious, executing a brilliant sequence of moves that had left his opponent with no choice but to concede.

The realization sent a chill down his spine. The killer wasn't just playing games—he was reenacting them, using the moves from Reynolds' own past as a blueprint for his crimes. The chess positions on the walls weren't just a message. They were a challenge, a twisted attempt to draw Reynolds into a deadly game of cat and mouse.

Reynolds stared at the final position in the sequence, the one painted so prominently on the wall. It was a checkmate, the move that had won him the championship. But here, in the context of the murders, it took on a far more sinister meaning.

The killer was declaring checkmate—not just on the board, but in the real world. And Reynolds was the opponent, the one being played.

The implications of this realization were staggering. If the killer was using chess as a metaphor for his crimes, then understanding the game could be the key to stopping him. Reynolds' past, his knowledge of the game, was suddenly more relevant than ever. The very skills he had once used to outmaneuver opponents on the chessboard could now be the key to outwitting a murderer.

Reynolds felt a surge of determination. He wasn't going to let the killer win this game. He would study the positions, analyze every move, and use his knowledge of chess to anticipate the killer's next steps. This wasn't just about solving a case anymore—it was personal.

The game was on, and this time, Reynolds was ready to play.

13

The Game Unfolds

Detective James Reynolds couldn't escape the images of the chess positions that had been haunting him ever since he saw them in that abandoned house. Each position painted in bold, crimson strokes taunted him, replaying in his mind over and over. They weren't just random patterns; there was a deliberate intent behind them, something that gnawed at his thoughts day and night.

Exhausted and desperate for answers, Reynolds returned to his office late one evening. The sun had long set, and the only light in the room came from the dim, flickering lamp on his desk. The shadows stretched across the room, adding to the oppressive atmosphere that seemed to have settled over him like a heavy blanket.

His office had become a sanctuary of sorts—a place where he could retreat from the world and lose himself in the chaos of the case. The walls were covered with maps, crime scene photos, and countless notes, all connected by a web of red string that crisscrossed the corkboard in a haphazard fashion. It was a mess, a visual representation of his scattered thoughts, but he couldn't tear his eyes away from it.

Reynolds sat heavily in his chair, his body aching from the long hours and lack of sleep. He stared at the corkboard, his mind racing. The locations of the murders were all there, marked by red pins, but no matter how hard he tried, he couldn't see the pattern. It was as if the answer was right in front of him, just out of reach.

He reached into his desk drawer and pulled out an old chessboard, one that had been gathering dust for years. It was a relic from a time when chess had been his world—when he had been a young man with dreams of championships and glory. He hadn't touched the board in years, but something compelled him to set it up now, as if the pieces themselves held the answers he sought.

As he placed the pieces on the board, the memory of the positions painted on the walls of the abandoned house flashed through his mind. He could see them clearly, each one seared into his thoughts. He began to arrange the pieces on the board, replicating the positions as best he could from memory.

For a moment, he simply stared at the board, his mind blank. The positions seemed familiar, yet foreign at the same time, like a half-remembered dream. He could feel the pieces of the puzzle slowly coming together, but there was still something missing—some crucial detail that eluded him.

Frustration bubbled up inside him, and he clenched his fists, his nails digging into his palms. How could he be so close, yet so far from the truth? The thought tormented him, driving him to the brink of madness.

And then, in a flash of clarity, it hit him.

Reynolds felt a chill run down his spine as the realization washed over him, cold and terrifying. The positions weren't just random. They were moves—moves from a chess game he knew all too well. His breath caught in his throat as he began to trace the sequence of the moves on the board, his hands trembling with a mixture of fear and disbelief.

Each move matched the locations of the murders perfectly. It was as if the killer had taken the game Reynolds had played years ago and brought it to life in the most horrifying way possible. The game wasn't just a game—it was a blueprint for murder, a twisted reenactment of his greatest victory.

He sat back in his chair, stunned. The implications of what he had discovered were almost too much to bear. The killer wasn't just playing a game with him—he was mocking him, using the very moves that had once brought him glory to bring about death and destruction. It was a cruel, twisted parody of everything Reynolds had once held dear.

His mind raced as he tried to make sense of it all. The final game of the national chess championship had been one of the proudest moments of his life, a moment when all his hard work and dedication had paid off. He had outmaneuvered his opponent with a series of brilliant moves, culminating in a checkmate that had sealed his victory.

But now, those same moves had become a weapon in the hands of a killer. The board before him was no longer just a chessboard—it was a map of death, each piece a symbol of a life taken. And the killer was playing him, using his own past against him in the most brutal way imaginable.

Reynolds felt his hands begin to shake as the full horror of the situation sank in. The killer had been following his every move, recreating the game with terrifying precision. But there was something even more disturbing—the killer was better than his opponent had been. The moves were executed with a level of skill and foresight that sent a shiver down Reynolds' spine.

He could feel the weight of the game pressing down on him, the stakes higher than they had ever been before. This wasn't just about solving a case anymore—it was a battle for his very soul, a battle against an opponent who knew him better than he knew himself.

Reynolds leaned forward, his eyes narrowing as he studied the board. The game wasn't over yet—there were still moves to be made. And if he could anticipate those moves, he might be able to stop the killer before it was too late.

He replayed the game in his mind, his thoughts moving at a frantic pace. The next move in the sequence would be crucial. If the killer was following the pattern, then there were only a few possible locations where the next murder could occur.

Reynolds felt a surge of determination as he placed the next move on the board. He scanned the map, matching the position with potential locations in the town. Three spots stood out to him, each one significant in its own way—places that held a certain resonance with the strategy of the game.

His heart pounded in his chest as he considered his options. He had to act quickly—there was no time to waste. The killer was out there, waiting to make his next move, and Reynolds knew that he had to be one step ahead.

But even as he mobilized his team, setting up surveillance at the three locations, a nagging doubt gnawed at the back of his mind. The killer had been playing him all along, manipulating the game to his own ends. What if this was just another trap, another move designed to throw him off balance?

Reynolds shook his head, pushing the doubt aside. He couldn't afford to hesitate, not now. The lives of innocent people were at stake, and he couldn't let the killer win.

The game was unfolding before him, each move bringing him closer to the final confrontation. Reynolds knew that he had to stay focused, had to keep his wits about him. The killer was a master of the game, but so was he. And this time, he was determined to come out on top.

As he prepared to leave his office and join his team at the stakeout, Reynolds took one last look at the chessboard. The pieces were set, the game in motion. But this wasn't just a game anymore—it was a matter of life and death.

The question was—could he outmaneuver the killer in time?

14

Anticipating the Next Move

The atmosphere in Detective Reynolds' office was heavy with anticipation. The chessboard on his desk had become the focal point of his life, each piece representing a murder, each move a step closer to understanding the mind of the killer. The realization that the murders mirrored the moves from his championship game had been a chilling revelation, but now he believed he was one step ahead—ready to prevent the next death.

He had identified three potential locations where the killer might strike, all corresponding to the next move in the game. The plan was in place, the team deployed. All that was left was to wait.

Reynolds sat in the unmarked car, his eyes fixed on the street outside. The night was cold and still, the silence broken only by the occasional rustle of leaves in the wind. He checked his watch—2:00 a.m. Time was slipping away, and with each passing minute, his anxiety grew.

Beside him, Deputy Sarah Miller sipped her coffee, her gaze drifting between the darkened buildings. She could sense the tension radiating from Reynolds, the way his fingers drummed restlessly on the steering wheel.

"We've got this, Sheriff," she said quietly, trying to reassure him. "We've covered all the bases."

Reynolds didn't respond immediately. His mind was racing, playing out the possibilities, the what-ifs. "I hope so," he finally muttered, though his tone betrayed his doubt. He couldn't shake the feeling that he was missing something—some critical detail that would make all the pieces fall into place.

The hours dragged on, the night stretching into the early hours of the morning. The cold seeped into the car, making Reynolds' muscles stiffen, but he barely noticed. His focus was absolute, his eyes scanning the street for any sign of movement.

But nothing happened.

No shadowy figure emerged from the darkness, no sudden sound shattered the silence. The night passed without incident, leaving Reynolds with a sinking feeling in the pit of his stomach. Something was wrong. The killer should have made a move by now. So why hadn't he?

"Maybe we got it wrong," Sarah said, breaking the silence. "Maybe he's waiting for another time, or maybe he's moved on to a different location."

Reynolds clenched his jaw, frustration boiling over. "We didn't get it wrong. This is the move. This is where he's supposed to strike."

But even as he said the words, doubt gnawed at him. What if he had been outmaneuvered? What if the killer was playing a different game entirely?

As dawn began to break, casting a pale light over the deserted streets, Reynolds received the call he had been dreading.

"Sheriff, we've got a situation," came the voice on the other end of the line, tense and urgent. "There's been another murder. But it wasn't at any of the locations we were watching."

Reynolds' heart sank as the words hit him like a physical blow. "Where?" he demanded, his voice harsh.

The address given was nowhere near the three locations they had staked out. It was a place that had never even crossed his mind—an old, abandoned warehouse on the outskirts of town, far removed from the game he thought he had been playing.

Reynolds' hands tightened on the steering wheel as he sped towards the new crime scene, his thoughts a chaotic jumble of fear and confusion. How had he missed this? How had the killer outsmarted him so completely?

When he arrived at the warehouse, the scene was eerily familiar. The crime scene tape, the flashing lights, the grim expressions on the faces of the officers—it was all too much like the other murders. But this time, the weight of failure pressed down on him like never before.

Reynolds stepped out of the car, his heart heavy as he approached the body. The victim, a young woman, lay crumpled on the cold concrete floor, her lifeless eyes staring up at the ceiling. The sight of her, so brutally murdered, sent a wave of guilt crashing over him. This was his fault. He had been so sure, so confident that he knew the killer's next move. And yet, here he was, standing over another victim, another life lost because he had been outplayed.

Sarah joined him, her face pale as she took in the scene. "How did this happen, Sheriff? We were so sure..."

Reynolds didn't answer. He couldn't. His mind was too consumed with the realization that he had been bested by a superior player—someone who had not only anticipated his moves but had manipulated him into thinking he was in control.

They finished their work at the scene and headed back to the station in silence. The weight of the night's failure hung heavily in the air, a palpable reminder of the stakes they were playing for. The drive back felt interminable, each minute stretching out as Reynolds replayed the events in his mind, searching for the mistake, the move he had missed.

Back at the station, Reynolds went straight to his office, barely acknowledging the other officers who greeted him. He slammed the door behind him, shutting out the world as he stared at the chessboard on his desk. It seemed mocking now, the pieces arranged in what had seemed like a winning strategy just hours before.

He moved to the corkboard on the wall where the murders were mapped out, and with trembling hands, he pinned the location of the latest murder in place. The map was a chaotic mess of red strings and photos, but as he stared at it, something clicked.

Reynolds returned to his desk, his eyes narrowing as he placed the latest murder on the chessboard. He studied the positions, his mind working furiously to understand the pattern. There was something he had missed—something subtle, but brilliant.

And then he saw it.

The killer had executed a move that his opponent in the championship had never made. It was a maneuver so subtle, so ingenious, that Reynolds hadn't even considered it. But now, as he stared at the board, the brilliance of the move was undeniable.

It wasn't just a move—it was a checkmate.

Reynolds sank into his chair, the realization hitting him like a punch to the gut. The killer wasn't just mimicking his past—he was improving on it. He was a superior player, someone who had taken Reynolds' greatest victory and twisted it into a deadly game.

The implications were staggering. This wasn't just about outmaneuvering a killer anymore. This was a battle of minds, a contest between two players who understood each other all too well. But the killer had the advantage—he was always one step ahead, always playing a different game.

Reynolds stared at the board, the pieces blurring before his eyes as the weight of the situation pressed down on him. He had been outplayed, outwitted, and now he was left scrambling to catch up, knowing that the next move could mean the difference between life and death.

The game had changed, and Reynolds knew that he had to change with it. The stakes were higher than ever, and if he wanted to win, he would have to be better—smarter, faster, more ruthless.

Because now, he was playing against a master.

15

The Grandmaster's Insight

Detective James Reynolds was at his wit's end. The realization that he had been outmaneuvered by a killer who seemed to anticipate his every move left him reeling. He knew that he was in over his head; the chess game that the killer was playing had reached a level of complexity that he could no longer navigate alone.

Desperation gnawed at him as he stared at the chessboard in his office, the pieces mocking him with their silent challenge. He needed help—someone who understood the game in ways he never could. And there was only one person who came to mind.

Reynolds picked up the phone and dialed a number he hadn't used in years. It rang a few times before a voice answered on the other end.

"Hello?"

"Grandmaster Valery Ivanov?" Reynolds asked, trying to keep the urgency out of his voice.

"Yes, this is Valery. Who is this?"

"It's James Reynolds," he replied. "We met a long time ago at the national championships. You might not remember me, but—"

"Detective Reynolds," Valery interrupted, his voice thoughtful. "Of course, I remember you. You were quite the player back in the day. What can I do for you?"

Reynolds hesitated for a moment, unsure of how to explain the bizarre situation. But there was no time for hesitation. "I need your help. It's about a case I'm working on... a series of murders. The killer is using chess as a blueprint for the crimes, and I've realized that he's following the moves from a game I played years ago."

There was a pause on the other end of the line, and Reynolds could almost hear the wheels turning in Valery's mind.

"That's... highly unusual," Valery finally said, his voice tinged with curiosity. "But I suppose it's not impossible. Chess can be a metaphor for many things, including life and death. What do you need from me?"

"I need you to look at the board," Reynolds said. "I'm out of options here. This killer is always one step ahead of me, and I can't anticipate his moves anymore. I was hoping you could help me figure out what he might do next."

Valery agreed to meet with Reynolds later that evening. The two men convened in Reynolds' office, the atmosphere tense and charged with the weight of the situation. Valery, a tall man with a shock of white hair and sharp, piercing eyes, looked every bit the chess grandmaster he was known to be. His presence commanded respect, and Reynolds couldn't help but feel a flicker of hope as the grandmaster sat down at the desk and surveyed the board.

"Let's see what we have here," Valery murmured, his eyes scanning the positions of the pieces with practiced precision.

Reynolds explained the situation as succinctly as he could, outlining the killer's strategy and the moves that had led to the murders. Valery listened intently, his brow furrowing in concentration as he absorbed the information.

When Reynolds finished, Valery leaned back in his chair, his expression thoughtful. "This is a very unusual case, Detective. It's clear that the killer is not just imitating your game—he's improving upon it. He's executing moves that are beyond the scope of ordinary play, moves that suggest a deep understanding of the game."

Reynolds nodded, feeling the weight of Valery's words. "That's what I was afraid of. I thought I could predict his next move, but he's always one step ahead. I need to know what he might do next."

Valery studied the board for a long moment, his fingers lightly touching the pieces as if he could feel the thought process of the killer through them. "There are a few possibilities," he said finally, his voice measured. "The killer has been following your game, but he's also been adapting, making moves that you never made. That suggests a higher level of play—he's not just copying you, he's challenging you."

Reynolds felt a cold knot of fear tighten in his chest. "So what does that mean? How do we stop him?"

"It means we have to think like him," Valery said, his tone serious. "We have to anticipate not just the obvious moves, but the subtle ones—the ones that require a deeper understanding of the game. For example, the killer could be planning a sacrifice—a move that might seem reckless or illogical at first, but could lead to a decisive advantage later on."

Reynolds stared at the board, trying to wrap his mind around the possibilities. "A sacrifice? But what would he gain from that?"

"Control," Valery replied simply. "A sacrifice can throw the opponent off balance, make them think they've gained the upper hand when in reality, they're walking into a trap."

Reynolds felt a shiver run down his spine. The idea of the killer sacrificing something—or someone—to gain control was terrifying. But it also made sense. The killer had already proven himself to be ruthlessly cunning, willing to do whatever it took to stay ahead.

Valery continued, pointing out several other possible moves the killer might make. Each one was more complex than the last, requiring a level of foresight and strategy that left Reynolds feeling overwhelmed. But he knew he couldn't afford to be overwhelmed—not now.

As Valery laid out the scenarios, Reynolds could feel a renewed sense of determination building within him. The stakes were higher than ever, but he wasn't alone in this anymore. With Valery's help, he might just have a chance to outmaneuver the killer, to anticipate his moves before it was too late.

But the pressure was immense. The lives of potential victims hinged on their ability to outthink a killer who had already proven to be a master strategist. One wrong move, one miscalculation, and it could all be over.

Valery finished his analysis and sat back, his sharp eyes meeting Reynolds'. "You have a formidable opponent, Detective. But remember, even the best players can make mistakes. The key is to stay focused, to anticipate his moves before he can make them."

As Valery studied the board one last time, he leaned forward, his eyes narrowing in concentration. "There are a few paths the killer might take from here, Detective," he said, his voice grave. "He could push aggressively with a direct attack—something bold, that catches you off guard. Or he might opt for a feint, a move that appears weak but is designed to lure you into a trap. And then there's the possibility of a quiet, subtle maneuver—positioning a piece in such a way that it doesn't seem threatening at first, but sets up a devastating strike several moves later. You need to be prepared for all of these, because each one carries a different kind of danger."

Valery leaned back, eyes still fixed on the board, before pointing to a few key positions. "Detective, based on the patterns I've observed and the way the killer has been playing, I see three possible moves he might make next—each corresponding to a location.

First, if he's aiming for a bold strike, he could target the old mill by the river. It's isolated, perfect for a quick, decisive action that leaves little room for response.

Second, if he's trying to draw you in with a feint, I'd watch the town square. It's a public area, and a move there would force you into a difficult position, trying to protect the most vulnerable while he prepares his next move.

And lastly, there's the quiet maneuver—the one that worries me most. The abandoned train station on the outskirts. It's a place no one would think to check immediately, giving him time to set up his next attack without raising suspicion."

Valery looked up, his expression stern. "These are the locations I'd keep an eye on, Detective. The killer's next move will likely be at one of these spots. Be ready, because whichever he chooses, it's going to be decisive."

Reynolds nodded, absorbing Valery's advice. "Thank you, Grandmaster. I couldn't have done this without you."

Valery smiled faintly. "Just remember, Detective, in chess—as in life—it's not about who makes the first move, but who makes the last."

Reynolds watched as Valery left his office, the weight of the case pressing down on him even more heavily now. The killer was playing a game, yes, but it was a game with real consequences, real lives at stake. And Reynolds knew that he couldn't afford to lose.

The chessboard in front of him was no longer just a game—it was a battlefield. And Reynolds was determined to win, no matter the cost.

9 798330 324187